# Play Ball!

by James Buckley, Jr.

photography by Mike Eliason

MAJOR LEAGUE BASEBALL

London, New York, Munich,
Melbourne, and Delhi

**Project Editor** Beth Sutinis
**Senior Art Editor** Michelle Baxter
**Publisher** Andrew Berkhut

**Produced by**
**Shoreline Publishing Group LLC**
Santa Barbara, California
**Editorial Director** James Buckley, Jr.
**Designer** Tom Carling, Carling Design, Inc.

Produced in partnership and licensed by
Major League Baseball Properties, Inc.
**Executive Vice President** Timothy J. Brosnan
**Vice President of Publishing** Don Hintze
Major League Baseball Properties, Inc.
245 Park Avenue, New York, NY 10167

First American Edition, 2002
03 04 05 10 9 8 7 6 5 4 3

Published in the United States by
DK Publishing, Inc.
375 Hudson Street
New York, New York 10014

DK Publishing, Inc. offers special discounts for bulk purchases for sales
promotions or premiums. Specific, large-quantity needs can be met
with special editions, including personalized covers, excerpts of existing
guides, and corporate imprints. For more information, contact
Special Markets Department, DK Publishing, Inc.,
375 Hudson Street, New York, New York 10014

Library of Congress Cataloging-in-Publication Data

Buckley, James, Jr.
    Play ball / by James Buckley, Jr. — 1st American ed.
        p.cm.
    Summary: Photographs and text, including tips from
professional players, show how to warm up, select the right
equipment, and play baseball.
    ISBN 0-7894-8509-5
    1. Baseball for children—Juvenile literature. 2. Baseball
for children—training—Juvenile literature. [1. Baseball.]
I. Title: Play Ball. II. Title.

GV880.4.B83 2002
796.357'2—dc21

2001047620

Reproduced by Colourscan, Ltd, Singapore
Printed and bound in Spain by Artes Graficas, Toledo, SA.
D.L. TO: 1381 - 2002

see our complete catalog at
**www.dk.com**

# Contents

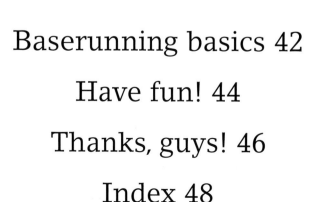

# Introduction

BASEBALL HAS BEEN AMERICA'S "National Pastime" since before the Civil War. The game grew out of other stick-and-ball games played in England. The first teams were formed under "modern" rules in the 1850s. From the beginning, kids were a part of the sport, playing in fields, sandlots, parks, and backyards. So as you head out to play with your team and your friends, you're carrying on a tradition that goes back more than 150 years.

The equipment the players used back then might have been only a small glove (if any!), scuffed balls, and wooden bats.

Today's players use leather gloves, wear plastic batting and catching helmets and other safety gear, and swing unbreakable aluminum bats.

But while some things are different, many others are the same. Young players still throw strikes, swing the bat, catch fly balls, field grounders, and slide into bases.

This book is designed to help young players learn more about the skills that kids of all ages have used since the game's earliest days. We hope that this book (and the cool tips from Major Leaguers!) help you carry on the tradition.

**The good old days?**
They didn't wear plastic batting helmets, but they played the same game you do.

# How To Use This Book

Every two-page "spread" in this book is packed with useful information. This diagram shows you the best way to read the book and find the tips you need to succeed.

Blue arrows show the path of a hand.

Inset photos give closeup looks.

Boldface "annotations" are used to help you focus attention on specific parts of each skill.

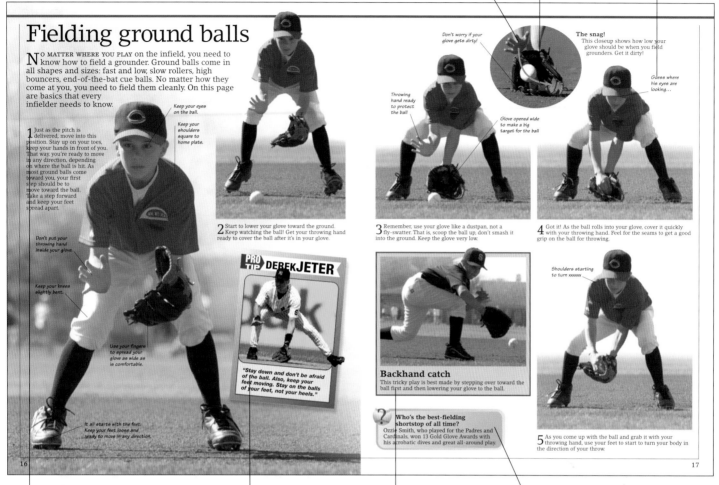

## Fielding ground balls

NO MATTER WHERE YOU PLAY on the infield, you need to know how to field a grounder. Ground balls come in all shapes and sizes: fast and low, slow rollers, high bouncers, end-of-the-bat cue balls. No matter how they come at you, you need to field them cleanly. On this page are basics that every infielder needs to know.

Keep your eyes on the ball.

Keep your shoulders square to home plate.

1 Just as the pitch is delivered, move into this position. Stay up on your toes, keep your hands in front of you. That way, you're ready to move in any direction, depending on where the ball is hit. As most ground balls come toward you, your first step should be to move toward the ball. Take a step forward and keep your feet spread apart.

Don't put your throwing hand inside your glove.

Keep your knees slightly bent.

Use your fingers to spread your glove as wide as is comfortable.

It all starts with the feet. Keep your feet loose and ready to move in any direction.

2 Start to lower your glove toward the ground. Keep watching the ball! Get your throwing hand ready to cover the ball after it's in your glove.

**PRO TIP DEREK JETER**

"Stay down and don't be afraid of the ball. Also, keep your feet moving. Stay on the balls of your feet, not your heels."

Don't worry if your glove gets dirty!

Throwing hand ready to protect the ball.

**The snag!** This closeup shows how low your glove should be when you field grounders. Get it dirty!

Glove opened wide to make a big target for the ball.

3 Remember, use your glove like a dustpan, not a fly-swatter. That is, scoop the ball up, don't smash it into the ground. Keep the glove very low.

**Backhand catch**
This tricky play is best made by stepping over toward the ball first and then lowering your glove to the ball.

**? Who's the best-fielding shortstop of all time?**
Ozzie Smith, who played for the Padres and Cardinals, won 13 Gold Glove Awards with his acrobatic dives and great all-around play.

Guess where his eyes are looking...

4 Got it! As the ball rolls into your glove, cover it quickly with your throwing hand. Feel for the seams to get a good grip on the ball for throwing.

Shoulders starting to turn xxxxxx

5 As you come up with the ball and grab it with your throwing hand, use your feet to start to turn your body in the direction of your throw.

16

17

Step-by-step photos are used to show key baseball skills. Follow the numbers in order across the pages.

Every spread contains a tip from a Major League player.

Tan boxes give a closer look at a baseball skill.

Look for baseball trivia, records, slang terms, and more in these green boxes.

# To Parents and Coaches:

First, thank you for your interest in your child and his or her enjoyment of baseball. The best way to encourage your child to continue in the sport is to emphasize the fun, teamwork, and togetherness of the game. Another way is to help them develop their skills. Playing well makes it easier to have fun.

The photographs and diagrams in this book are designed to give a very basic and simple introduction to the key baseball skills of fielding, throwing, pitching, batting, playing catcher, and baserunning. As you know, there is much more to the game than these basic skills, and we thank you for helping your kids continue their baseball education through practices and games, and by just being there to play catch with them.

Of course, another way to share the game with your kids is to watch baseball with them. Whether that is Major League Baseball in person or on TV or a local college or high school game, there is nothing like seeing the game in person to help generate excitement about playing it.

Helping your child play in an organized league is a great way to help them get started. Most leagues are broken up into age brackets so that children play with kids of similar abilities and sizes. Your local parks and recreation department—or other parents—can help you find the league in your area. Kids don't necessarily need a league to enjoy baseball, but the structure and supervision certainly makes it easier for them and for parents. (Plus, of course, they love to wear uniforms!)

One important safety note: While we all want baseball to be fun, we also want the players to be safe. Make sure your child wears proper safety gear while batting, that they have baseball shoes or sneakers that fit properly, and they understand safety when swinging a bat.

Again, thanks for your interest. We hope that you enjoy this book with your young ballplayers. —J.B.

# Play ball!

$S$INCE THE FIRST GAMES in the 1840s, the rules of baseball have remained pretty much the same. The rules would be just as familiar to a kid from 100 years ago: nine players, nine innings in a game, three outs per inning per team. Batters try to reach base, while fielders try to stop them.

## In the zone

The game starts with a pitcher throwing to a batter. The pitcher tries to put the ball in the strike zone, shown by the red box below. The batter chooses a pitch to hit, and if he puts in fair territory, he drops the bat and runs like heck to first base!

*Youth players use aluminum bats, which don't break as easily as wood bats.*

*Batters stand on one side of home plate to await the pitch.*

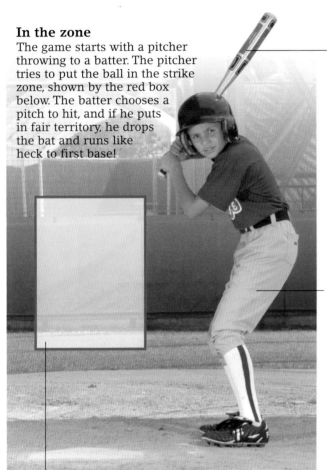

*The strike zone is an imaginary box over home plate that stretches from chest to knees.*

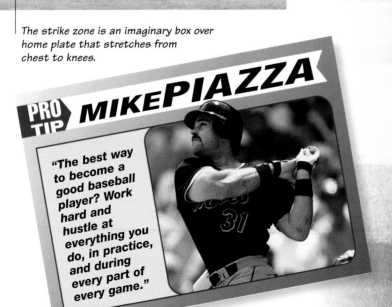

### PRO TIP — MIKE PIAZZA

"The best way to become a good baseball player? Work hard and hustle at everything you do, in practice, and during every part of every game."

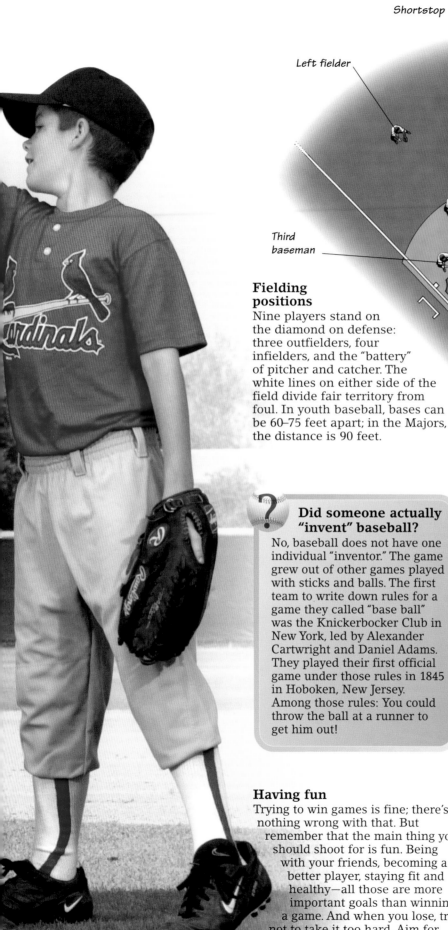

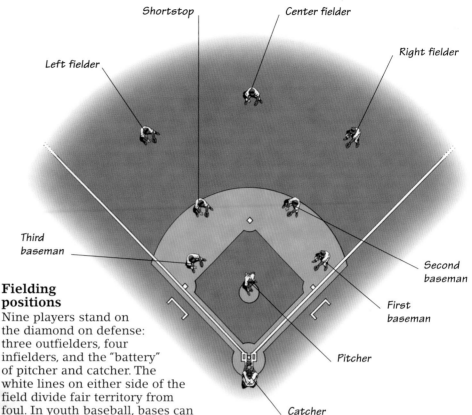

Shortstop

Center fielder

Right fielder

Left fielder

Third baseman

Second baseman

First baseman

Pitcher

Catcher

## Fielding positions

Nine players stand on the diamond on defense: three outfielders, four infielders, and the "battery" of pitcher and catcher. The white lines on either side of the field divide fair territory from foul. In youth baseball, bases can be 60–75 feet apart; in the Majors, the distance is 90 feet.

### ? Did someone actually "invent" baseball?

No, baseball does not have one individual "inventor." The game grew out of other games played with sticks and balls. The first team to write down rules for a game they called "base ball" was the Knickerbocker Club in New York, led by Alexander Cartwright and Daniel Adams. They played their first official game under those rules in 1845 in Hoboken, New Jersey. Among those rules: You could throw the ball at a runner to get him out!

## Having fun

Trying to win games is fine; there's nothing wrong with that. But remember that the main thing you should shoot for is fun. Being with your friends, becoming a better player, staying fit and healthy—all those are more important goals than winning a game. And when you lose, try not to take it too hard. Aim for fun and you'll always be a winner.

## Scoring runs

The object of the game is to advance baserunners around the bases by hitting the ball. After a runner has touched first, second, and third (in order!), he touches home plate (above) to score a run for his team. The team with the most runs wins.

# Gearing up

Your cap should fit snugly, not too loose or too tight.

Keep your team jersey clean and ready for game day!

Some baseball pants need a belt, but most youth pants just have elastic waistbands.

Players often wear special baseball pants that end just below the knee.

Baseball "stirrup" socks come in many forms; here the stripe is sewn into the sock itself. Some players wear a separate colored stirrup over white socks.

Young players should wear shoes with plastic molded cleats for safety and to get a good grip on the field.

**B**EFORE YOU TAKE THE FIELD, you need to get the right baseball gear. Your coach or league will probably provide the team jersey and hat, but you'll have to do the rest. The key pieces of gear are your glove and shoes. Many gloves come from the store ready to play, but playing catch with it will help make the glove looser and more comfortable. As for baseball cleats, choose a pair that fit you now, not ones you'll grow into. The wrong size cleats can give you blisters. Baseball pants are a good thing to wear and will make your team really look like big leaguers, even if they do feel sort of odd at first.

## PRO TIP  CAL RIPKEN

"Pick a bat that feels right to you. Make sure you can control it using a good, short swing. Take some practice swings with it to see if it feels right."

### Nomar says: "Don't touch my glove!"

Major League players can be superstitious about their gear. Red Sox shortstop Nomar Garciaparra won't let anyone pick up or put their hand into his glove. "I take care of my glove and it takes care of me," he says.

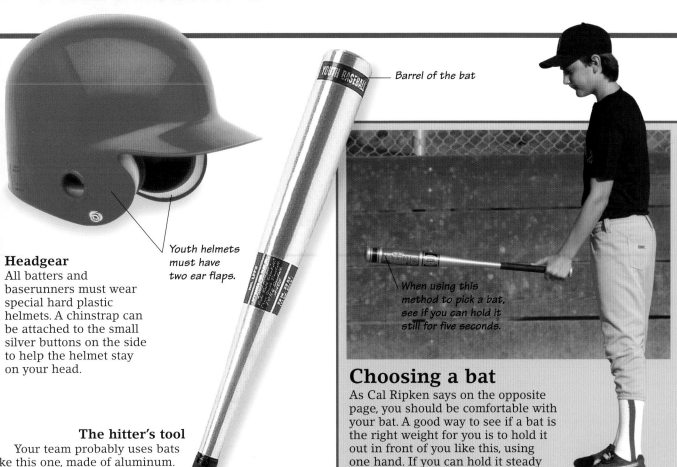

Barrel of the bat

## Headgear
All batters and baserunners must wear special hard plastic helmets. A chinstrap can be attached to the small silver buttons on the side to help the helmet stay on your head.

*Youth helmets must have two ear flaps.*

*When using this method to pick a bat, see if you can hold it still for five seconds.*

## Choosing a bat
As Cal Ripken says on the opposite page, you should be comfortable with your bat. A good way to see if a bat is the right weight for you is to hold it out in front of you like this, using one hand. If you can hold it steady without too much effort, it's the right weight for you.

## The hitter's tool
Your team probably uses bats like this one, made of aluminum. If your coach doesn't provide bats, sporting goods stores usually offer a wide range of styles and prices. After you've picked the right one (see box), remember safety whenever you are swinging it. Check behind you before you take even one practice swing, and never throw your bat, which could damage it—or someone standing nearby!

*Bat handle, wrapped in rubber for a good grip*

*Leather gloves are best and come in many styles and colors.*

## Can't play without it!
Your coach and league will provide baseballs for you that are an appropriate size for your age. Ever wonder what's inside a baseball? Hundreds of yards of wool are wrapped around a center of cork and rubber.

*Gloves are available with a wide variety of types of webbing.*

EASY CATCH

*Raised stitches on a baseball help players grip and throw it.*

Pocket

EZ CATCH™

Wilson®

## Flashing leather
Whether you are righthanded or lefthanded, choose a baseball glove that is not too big for your hand and that you can close easily around a ball. Take good care of it by keeping it clean and dry. Treat your glove right, and it will help you play your best.

Wrist strap

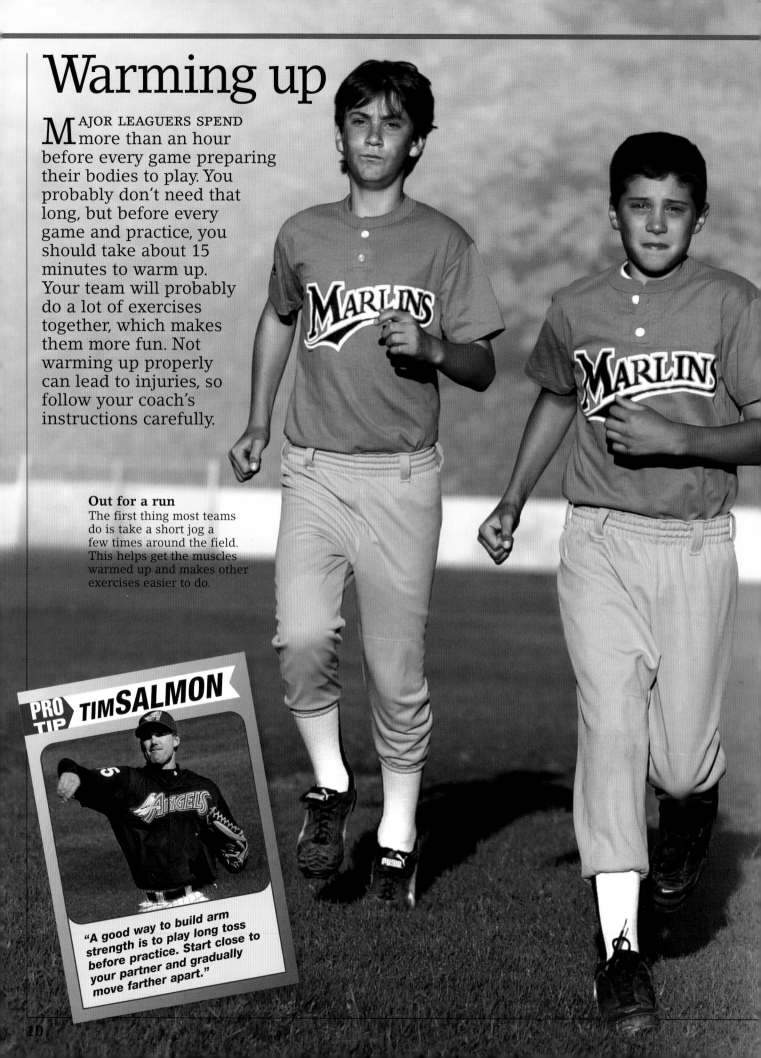

# Warming up

MAJOR LEAGUERS SPEND more than an hour before every game preparing their bodies to play. You probably don't need that long, but before every game and practice, you should take about 15 minutes to warm up. Your team will probably do a lot of exercises together, which makes them more fun. Not warming up properly can lead to injuries, so follow your coach's instructions carefully.

**Out for a run**
The first thing most teams do is take a short jog a few times around the field. This helps get the muscles warmed up and makes other exercises easier to do.

**PRO TIP › TIMSALMON**

"A good way to build arm strength is to play long toss before practice. Start close to your partner and gradually move farther apart."

## Water break

During any game or practice, don't be afraid to drink as much water as you need, especially on hotter days. Sports drinks are fine, too, but water is the best sports drink there is.

**"That guy's just a five o'clock hitter."**

Pros who do great during batting practice ("B.P.") and then not so well in games are called five o'clock hitters because B.P. is often held at that time.

## Just playing catch

The easiest and most fun pregame exercise is just playing catch. Start about half the distance from home to first. Throw easy at first then gradually throw harder.

## Warming up the wings

To stretch each shoulder, reach back over the other shoulder, keeping your arm level. Then slowly push on your elbow with your other hand. This player shows how to stretch both arms.

*Push easily with your hand on your elbow; don't force your arm back.*

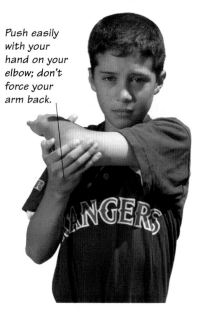

## Get those wheels ready

This hurdler's stretch is good for the hamstrings at the back of your leg and the quadriceps on the front of your thigh. Remember to stretch evenly and slowly; don't bounce.

# Throwing basics

THROWING IS THE most basic baseball skill, and it's also one of the easiest to master. This does not mean pitching to a batter; we mean just basic, accurate throwing. With practice, you'll develop your own style, but there are some basic tips on this page to help you throw better. No matter how many tips you get from this book or from coaches or Major Leaguers, the best way to become better at throwing a baseball is to just get out there and throw.

Ball rolls off your fingers when your hand is at the highest point

Keep your eyes on your target at all times.

As you throw, your chest will turn to face the target, too.

### Get a grip!
When you have time after making a catch, the best way to throw the ball to another player is to grip the ball with two fingers across the seams, as shown. The raised stitches help you hold the ball until you release it. By rolling the ball out of your hand and off your fingers, you create backspin, which helps your throws go straight and be more accurate.

PRO TIP ROBIN**VENTURA**

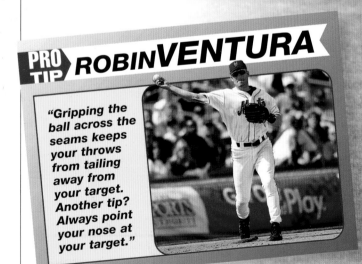

"Gripping the ball across the seams keeps your throws from tailing away from your target. Another tip? Always point your nose at your target."

Push off with your back foot as you step forward.

Step forward with the foot opposite your throwing hand.

# Side View of a Throw

This player throws righthanded. Imagine the pictures in reverse (or hold the page up to a mirror!) if you throw lefthanded.

*Like Robin Ventura says, point your nose at your target.*

*Your non-throwing arm can be held out to help you stay balanced.*

*Try not to bend or lean too far forward yet. Keep standing tall.*

**1** After getting a good grip on the ball, pull your throwing arm back and begin stepping toward your target. Point your non-throwing shoulder at your target as your hand goes back.

**2** Bring your forearm up vertically as you move your elbow forward. Your weight is now shifting from your back foot to your front foot.

**3** Keep pulling your elbow forward; your forearm and hand will follow. Your chest also begins to turn toward your target and your weight is all on your front leg.

*Try to have your elbow "pull" your arm and hand past your head.*

*Try to keep your back straight—don't bend over forward.*

*Even though you've released the ball, practice keeping your eye on the target.*

**4** As your elbow keeps moving forward, start to cock your wrist backward and push your forearm forward toward the target.

**5** When your elbow has gone as far as it can, your forearm whips around, almost perpendicular to the ground. Try to feel the ball rolling off your fingers as you release it.

**6** Snap your wrist slightly to give the ball good backspin. Follow through completely and smoothly. The more throwing you do, the better and more natural it will be for you.

13

# Types of throws

FIELDERS USE MANY DIFFERENT types of throws to get the ball where they want. No matter what style you use, remember that the best throw is the one that hits the target! This page shows the basic outfield throw after charging a ground ball (Rangers player), and a sidearm throw often used by infielders (Reds player).

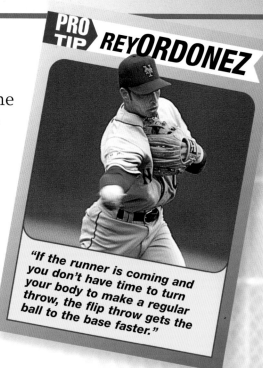

## OUTFIELD THROW

With runners on base, here is how outfielders should charge ground balls, scoop them up, and throw them to the base or cutoff man.

*Don't watch the baserunners, watch the baseball go into your glove.*

**1** Outfielders can get more power on their throws by charging balls hit in front of them. Keep your eyes down and your glove low as you scoop up the ball.

*Make a quick glance at your glove to help grab the ball, then look up.*

**2** Keep moving forward as you begin to reach for the ball in your glove. Start looking ahead to your target.

*As you hop, turn your front shoulder so it's pointed at the target.*

**3** Pro players call this the "crow hop." Jump slightly forward so you land on the foot that will be your back foot when you throw. Keep moving forward, grab the ball, and spot your target.

*Turn your chest toward the target.*

### The flip throw

A special throw that second basemen or shortstops sometimes use when close to the base is the underhand, or "flip" throw. When trying to turn a double play, you can shovel the ball more quickly to the base using this method than taking the time to step and throw overhand. After fielding, turn toward the base and toss the ball so your teammate catches it about chest high.

*Step directly at the target base.*

### Infield sidearm throw

Some infielders, usually shortstops, don't have much time to get the ball to the first baseman. To save time, they can use a quicker, sidearm throw like the one shown here. The player makes a shorter step and doesn't bring his arm as far back. He also whips his throwing arm forward a little faster, using more shoulder action than elbow action.

*The throwing arm is parallel to the shoulders.*

*In this throw, the elbow is straight, not bent.*

*See how the ball rolls off his fingers, even though his arm is lower than usual.*

*With your chest facing the target, reach up and fire the ball in. On outfield throws, your arm will be more vertical than it will on other throws.*

*Use your non-throwing arm for balance.*

5 Release the ball higher over your head than you would with a normal throw. Really try to feel your whole body pushing you and the ball toward your target.

*Look how close together his feet are when making this quicker throw.*

4 Plant your back foot firmly, and start pulling your arm back behind you. By moving forward, your whole body is helping make the throw.

# Fielding ground balls

No matter where you play on the infield, you need to know how to field a grounder. Ground balls come in all shapes and sizes: fast and low, slow rollers, high bouncers, end-of-the-bat cue balls. No matter how they come at you, you need to field them cleanly. On this page are the basics that every infielder needs to know.

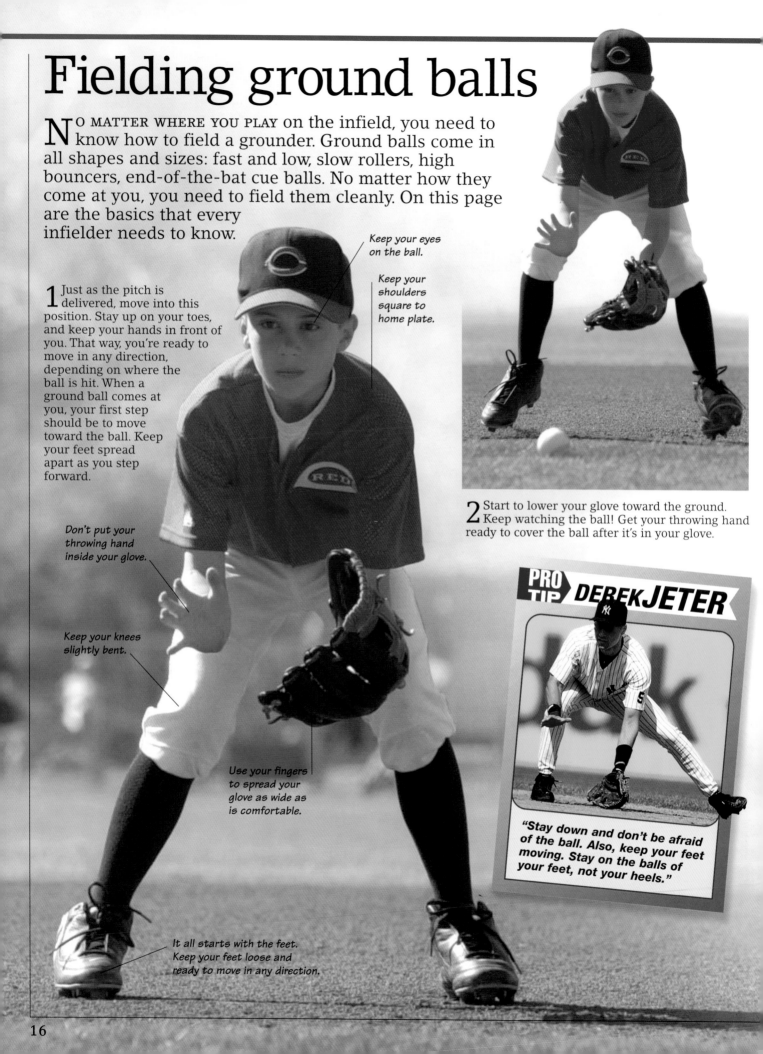

**1** Just as the pitch is delivered, move into this position. Stay up on your toes, and keep your hands in front of you. That way, you're ready to move in any direction, depending on where the ball is hit. When a ground ball comes at you, your first step should be to move toward the ball. Keep your feet spread apart as you step forward.

Keep your eyes on the ball.

Keep your shoulders square to home plate.

Don't put your throwing hand inside your glove.

Keep your knees slightly bent.

Use your fingers to spread your glove as wide as is comfortable.

It all starts with the feet. Keep your feet loose and ready to move in any direction.

**2** Start to lower your glove toward the ground. Keep watching the ball! Get your throwing hand ready to cover the ball after it's in your glove.

**PRO TIP** **DEREK JETER**

"Stay down and don't be afraid of the ball. Also, keep your feet moving. Stay on the balls of your feet, not your heels."

Don't worry if your glove gets dirty.

**The snag!**
This closeup shows how low your glove should be when you field grounders. Get it dirty!

Throwing hand ready to protect the ball

Glove opened wide to make a big target for the ball

Guess where his eyes are looking...

3 Remember, use your glove like a dustpan, not a fly-swatter. That is, scoop the ball up, don't smash it into the ground. Keep the glove very low.

4 Got it! As the ball rolls into your glove, cover it quickly with your throwing hand. Feel for the seams to get a good grip on the ball for throwing.

## Backhand catch
This tricky play is best made by stepping over toward the ball first and then lowering your glove to the ball.

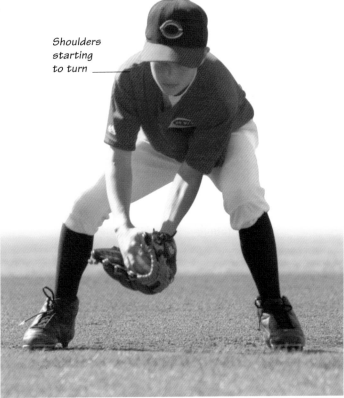

Shoulders starting to turn

**Who's the best-fielding shortstop of all time?**
Ozzie Smith, who played for the Padres and Cardinals, won 13 Gold Glove Awards with his acrobatic dives and great all-around play.

5 As you come up with the ball and grab it with your throwing hand, use your feet to start to turn your body in the direction of your throw.

# Catching fly balls

TRACKING DOWN FLY BALLS and catching them without getting hit on the head is one of the toughest things for many young players to learn. Practice will certainly help, along with these tips. The key is to learn to run to the spot where the ball will land and then catch it. Sounds simple, right? But it takes a lot of practice. During practice, try to catch balls hit in front of you and to the side, as well as over your head. The fielder shown here is lefthanded. Reverse these directions if you're righthanded.

*Keep your head up and your eyes on the ball.*

*Some players use gloves with holes for their index fingers.*

*Tuck your glove in as you run so that it doesn't slow you down.*

**1** This outfielder has just seen a ball hit over his head and to his left. His first move is to do a cross-over step with his right leg.

*Turn both feet in the direction of the ball and run. Don't backpedal.*

**2** As you arrive at the spot where you believe the ball will land, start to bring your glove hand and throwing hand up. Keep watching the ball!

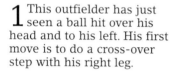

**PRO TIP JOHNNY DAMON**

*"When balls are hit over your head, start running first. Don't put up your glove until you're ready to catch it. It slows you down to run with your arm stuck out."*

## Two hands!

You won't see pros use two hands as often as they should, but that's the way young players should catch fly balls. Keep your arms bent at the elbow as the ball comes down and your glove above your head. Look for the ball over the top of the glove. As it hits the glove, cover it with your other hand.

*Start to open up your mitt as wide as you can to make a big target.*

*Put up your throwing hand to help you keep balanced.*

## Sun block
Keep your glove between your eyes and the sun. The ball will be a dark spot in the bright sky.

*Cover the ball and your glove with your throwing hand.*

**3** Here comes the ball! Watch it all the way into your mitt. Try to spot the ball just above your mitt, which should be above your head, not completely covering your face.

**4** The moment of truth. On this ball hit over his head, the fielder is still moving his feet to get into position when the ball drops. On balls hit right at you, try to have the foot on the glove side in front.

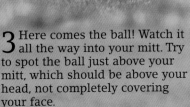
*Stay on your toes even as you're catching it, so you can react quickly.*

**5** As the ball slaps into your mitt, quickly close the mitt around it, then reach up with your throwing hand to cover it.

# Infield position basics

THE FOUR INFIELD POSITIONS ARE first base, second base, third base, and shortstop. All four players field ground balls and fly balls, make throws to bases, and make tag plays. However, each position does have its own special techniques that are used more often than at other positions. Take a trip around the diamond, and get some inside tips on how to be a better infielder.

*Stretch out as the throw is coming. Make a good target for your teammate.*

*Move toward the ball, but keep your body and glove low.*

## Go get it!
When playing the infield, charge toward ground balls hit right to you. By moving forward to meet the ball, you give yourself more time to throw the runner out.

*This player is standing up straight and stiff. He should be low and loose.*

*Keep your throwing hand away from your glove for balance.*

*Keep your eyes on the ball, not the runner.*

*Stay low so you can get the tag down quickly.*

*Keep your glove up and ready to make the catch.*

## Tag plays: right and wrong
Middle infielders—shortstops and second basemen—often have to make tag plays at second. The picture on the right shows the proper way to wait for the throw. The picture on the far right shows the wrong way. Stay off the base, straddling it with your feet. Keep your knees bent, stay on your toes, and be ready to move quickly to get the throw. If the throw isn't on target, forget the runner and be sure to catch the ball.

*On tag plays, the middle infielder should not act like a first baseman. Keep your foot OFF the base.*

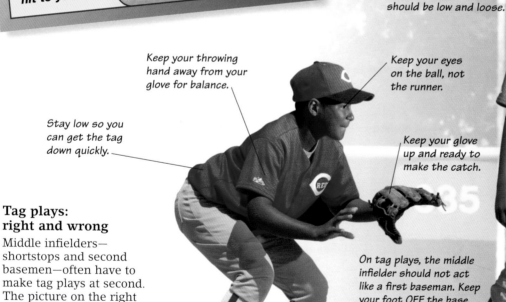

**RIGHT WAY**

**WRONG WAY**

**Playing first base**
Your most important job is catching throws from other infielders and stepping on the base to make an out. Keep the foot opposite your glove hand on the base. "Make a nice target for your teammate with your glove," says Eric Karros of the Los Angeles Dodgers. "Don't stretch for the throw until you see it coming."

*Always watch the teammate who is throwing you the ball; don't watch the baserunner.*

**The hot corner**
Third base is called that because many balls are hit hard toward this infielder who stands closer to the batter than other infielders. The key to success is to be in this ready position.

*Keep your eyes up.*

*Keep your glove down.*

**On the grass**
In bunt situations, third basemen often play closer to home plate, on the grass. Step forward as the pitch is thrown, and stay low to the ground and on your toes.

*Stretch out as the throw is coming; make a good target.*

*Don't step directly on the base; step on the corner, or keep the side of your foot next to the base.*

# Playing outfield

Outfielders cover a lot of grass. There are only three of you out there and lots of room for the ball to land. One of the hardest things about playing outfield is staying ready. Several innings might go by without the ball coming your way, but that doesn't mean it won't be hit at you on the very next pitch. To stay alert, pretend that every ball is hit to you and think about what you'd do if it was. Be ready at all times!

## Fielding ground balls

If there is no one on base or if you know you won't have to throw the ball right away, this is the best and safest way for outfielders to field ground balls. When the ball is hit to you, move forward to meet it. As it reaches you, put one knee on the ground.

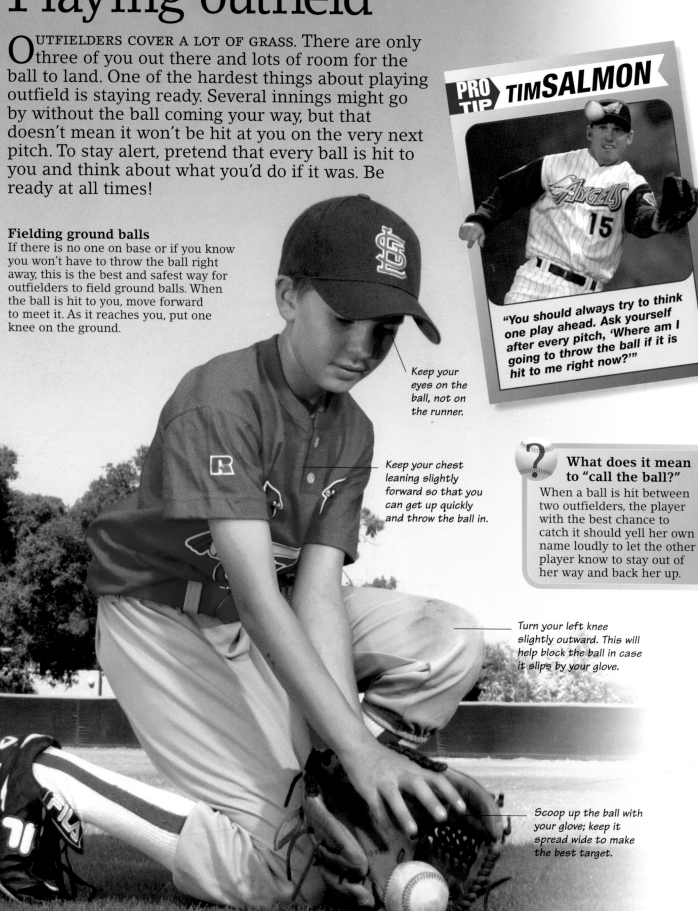

**PRO TIP** **TIM SALMON**

"You should always try to think one play ahead. Ask yourself after every pitch, 'Where am I going to throw the ball if it is hit to me right now?'"

Keep your eyes on the ball, not on the runner.

Keep your chest leaning slightly forward so that you can get up quickly and throw the ball in.

**? What does it mean to "call the ball?"**
When a ball is hit between two outfielders, the player with the best chance to catch it should yell her own name loudly to let the other player know to stay out of her way and back her up.

Turn your left knee slightly outward. This will help block the ball in case it slips by your glove.

Scoop up the ball with your glove; keep it spread wide to make the best target.

## Back up your teammates

It might not always seem like it, but you're not alone out there in the outfield. No matter where the ball is hit, outfielders should work together to back each other up. For instance, in the diagram the centerfielder has moved quickly toward a ball hit into right-centerfield, while the rightfielder has moved into backup position behind the centerfielder. Outfielders should not only back up each other, but infielders, too. Even on ground balls in the infield, outfielders should charge in behind, just in case the ball gets through.

*Back up your teammates even if it looks like an easy play.*

*Run into position behind your teammate while keeping your eyes on the ball.*

## Outfield shifts

One way to help make plays in the outfield is to move around depending on the type of batter at the plate. Your coach will help position you, but these two diagrams show basic shifts for left- and righthanded batters. Why shift? Here's an example: Lefthanded batters are likely to "pull" the ball toward rightfield. So if the outfielders move toward right field, they might be in better position to make a play.

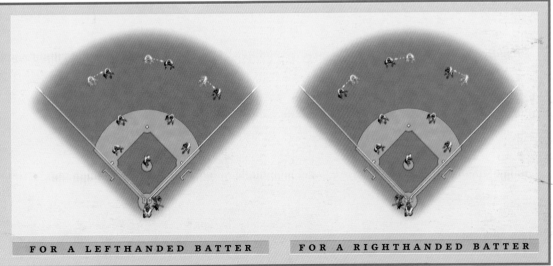

FOR A LEFTHANDED BATTER      FOR A RIGHTHANDED BATTER

# Cutoff plays

**D**EFENSE IS A TEAM GAME. Learning to work together with your teammates means outs and wins. An important team defense play is the cutoff, or relay, play. When a ball is hit to the outfield, the outfielder often throws the ball to an infielder who relays it to a base.

*Keep your shoulders square to the line between the outfielder and the base.*

*Be ready to turn in either direction if the throw is off line.*

**Key**
- LF to home
- Left-center to home
- CF to home
- Right-center to home
- RF to 3B
- RF to home

**Cutoff diagram**
This diagram shows some of the basic relays between outfielders and infielders. Use the color key at left to read it.

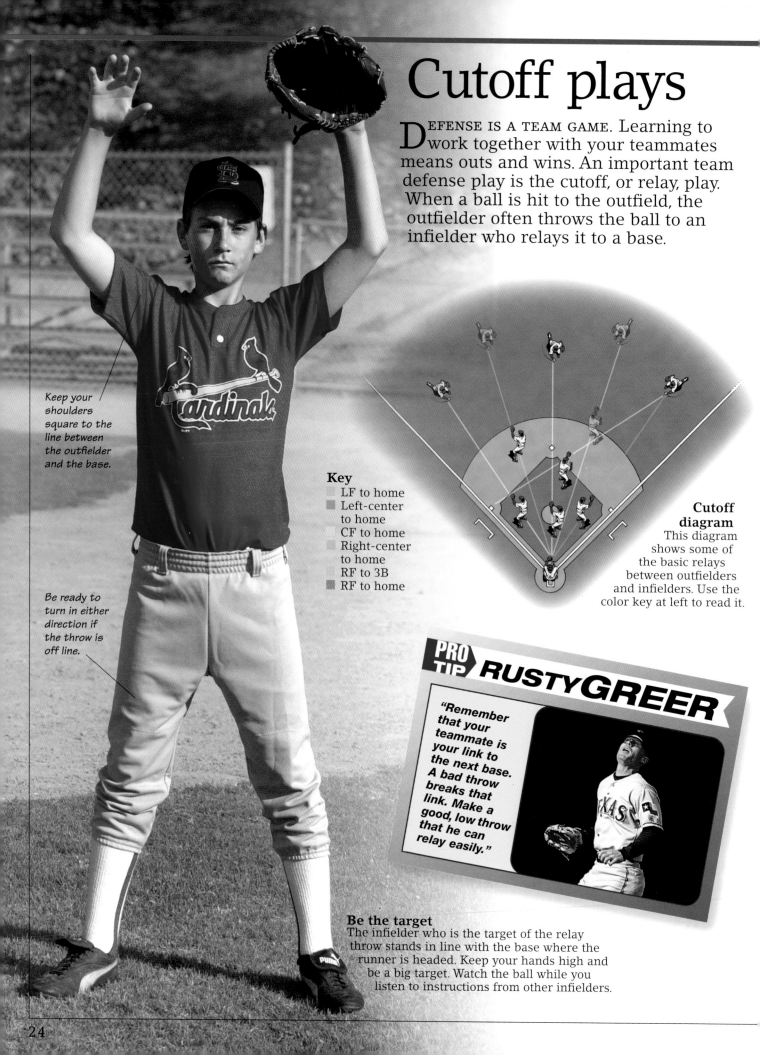

## PRO TIP **RustyGREER**

*"Remember that your teammate is your link to the next base. A bad throw breaks that link. Make a good, low throw that he can relay easily."*

**Be the target**
The infielder who is the target of the relay throw stands in line with the base where the runner is headed. Keep your hands high and be a big target. Watch the ball while you listen to instructions from other infielders.

# FROM OUTFIELD TO INFIELD

Practice making relay throws that help the infielder turn and throw in one motion, saving valuable time.

*Keep your arms up and your eyes on your teammate.*

*Outfielders should make low throws, not loops or arcs.*

**1** After the outfielder gets the ball, he should find his target man and step into a good, low throw. The infielder should line up between the base and the outfielder.

*As you catch the ball, start turning toward the infield.*

**2** The infielder catches the throw and starts to turn. If he has lined up with the base properly, he won't have to search for a target; he'll be pointed right at it as he turns in.

*Quickly pull your arm back and get ready to throw.*

**3** Try to catch the ball and throw in one motion. "Every step you take to throw is two steps that a baserunner is advancing," says Darin Erstad of the Anaheim Angels.

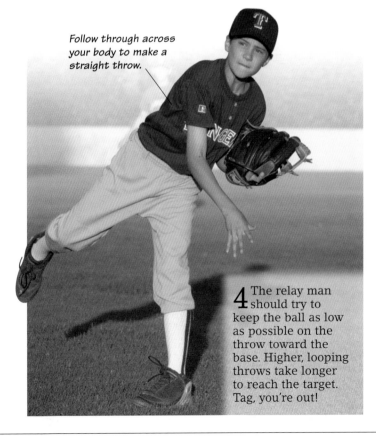

*Follow through across your body to make a straight throw.*

**4** The relay man should try to keep the ball as low as possible on the throw toward the base. Higher, looping throws take longer to reach the target. Tag, you're out!

# Playing catcher

CATCHER IS PROBABLY BASEBALL'S toughest position to play. Catchers wear more gear than any player, they spend most of the game squatting down, they get hit by foul tips and wild pitches, and they have to protect the plate against runners. Catcher is also one of the most important positions; often a good catcher can make the difference between a win and a loss for a team. And catchers are involved on every play, so they know they'll never be bored!

**PRO TIP** **MIKE PIAZZA**

"Give your pitcher a good low target in the strike zone. If your pitcher has confidence that you are setting a good target, he'll be comfortable."

*Keep your head up; don't bend forward with your neck.*

*Always keep your eyes on the pitcher and the pitch.*

*Try to keep your back straight, not rounded, as you crouch.*

*Pointing the glove up gives a good target and makes it easy to catch any pitch.*

*As the pitcher goes into her windup, move up onto your toes.*

## Put it right here!

Hall-of-Fame manager Casey Stengel once said, "You've gotta have a catcher. Otherwise, the ball rolls to the backstop." A catcher's first job is to catch pitches. By squatting down, you create a nice, low target for your pitcher. Try to find a comfortable stance that works for you. Keep your shoulders square to the field. Set your feet slightly wider than your shoulders. Most catchers keep their throwing hand behind them and use one hand to catch.

**FRONT VIEW**

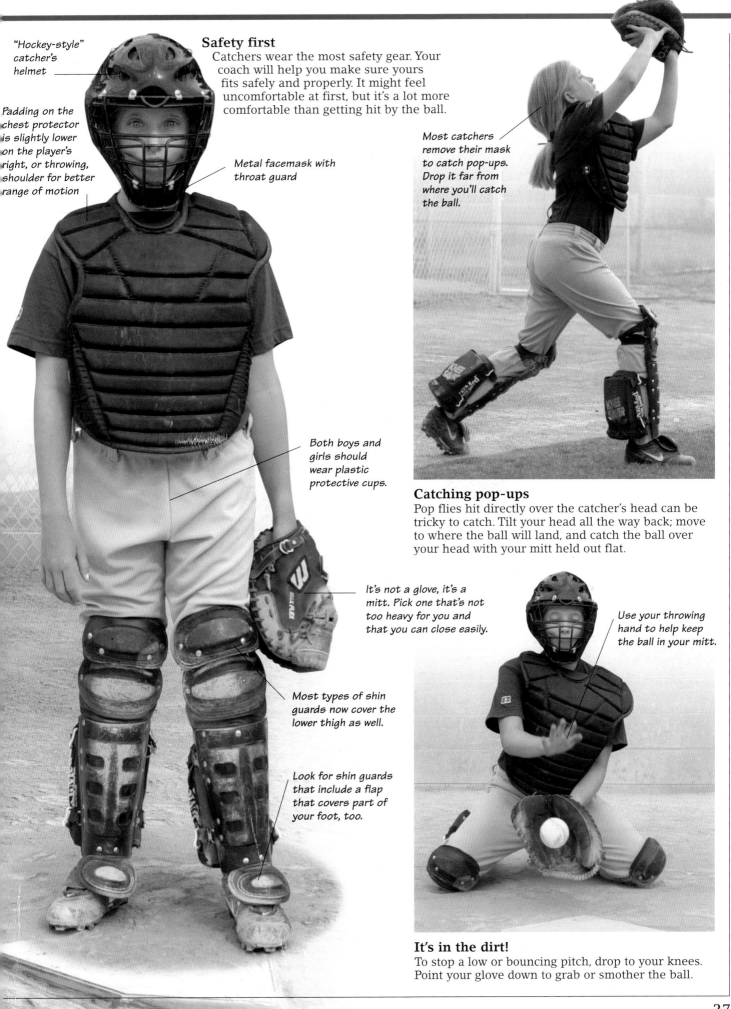

"Hockey-style" catcher's helmet

Padding on the chest protector is slightly lower on the player's right, or throwing, shoulder for better range of motion

### Safety first
Catchers wear the most safety gear. Your coach will help you make sure yours fits safely and properly. It might feel uncomfortable at first, but it's a lot more comfortable than getting hit by the ball.

Metal facemask with throat guard

Most catchers remove their mask to catch pop-ups. Drop it far from where you'll catch the ball.

Both boys and girls should wear plastic protective cups.

### Catching pop-ups
Pop flies hit directly over the catcher's head can be tricky to catch. Tilt your head all the way back; move to where the ball will land, and catch the ball over your head with your mitt held out flat.

It's not a glove, it's a mitt. Pick one that's not too heavy for you and that you can close easily.

Use your throwing hand to help keep the ball in your mitt.

Most types of shin guards now cover the lower thigh as well.

Look for shin guards that include a flap that covers part of your foot, too.

### It's in the dirt!
To stop a low or bouncing pitch, drop to your knees. Point your glove down to grab or smother the ball.

# Catching tips

A CATCHER'S JOB DOESN'T END with receiving pitches. Catchers make tag plays at home, and, in many youth leagues, must also try to throw out potential base stealers. A key skill for catchers is concentration; more than any other player on the field, you have to keep your head in the game.

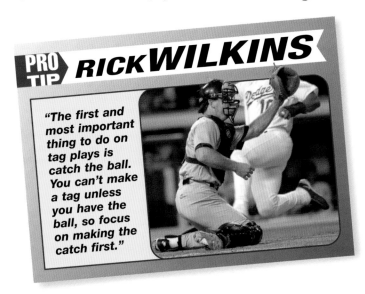

**PRO TIP** RICK**WILKINS**

*"The first and most important thing to do on tag plays is catch the ball. You can't make a tag unless you have the ball, so focus on making the catch first."*

## Blocking the plate

Catchers have to make tag plays at home plate. Stand in front of the plate, a step up the third-base line with your feet spread apart. Keep your eye on the ball first and the runner second. Hold your glove closed with your throwing hand to make the tag.

## THROWING TO SECOND

When a baserunner takes off from first to try to steal second base, a quick throw is as important as an accurate one. The steps in these photos show how a catcher must pop up from the crouch to throw.

*Watch the target, not the ball. Practice grabbing the ball without looking at it.*

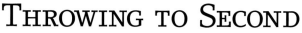

*Throwing hand moves to meet the mitt*

*Square your shoulders to the target as quickly as you can.*

**1** Everything happens at once when a runner takes off. As soon as the pitch hits your mitt, start standing up.

**2** Hop quickly so that your back foot moves into throwing position, while your hand grabs for the ball.

**3** Take a shorter step than on a normal throw. Keep your arm close to your body, and throw from behind your ear.

**What catcher has baseball's "best arm"?**

Texas Ranger catcher Ivan [ee-VON] Rodriguez has what many experts call the best throwing arm for a catcher in baseball history! He has won nine Gold Gloves. He not only has a great peg to second, but he has picked players off first base, too!

"Pounce like a cat," the pros say when a bunt falls to the ground near home plate. Getting there quickly gives you time to throw.

*Turn your shoulders toward your target before you throw.*

*Stay on your toes so you can move into throwing position easily.*

*Look at the ball, not the runner. If you drop it, he'll be safe.*

*Cock your wrist to create backspin.*

*As with any throw, keep your eyes on the target.*

**1** It is often easier to pick up the ball with your bare hand instead of using your glove.

**2** Make sure you have the ball securely, then turn to make a good throw to first base.

*Keep your glove hand in front of you for balance.*

*A good follow-through helps you learn a good throwing motion.*

*Keeping your back straight will keep your throws level.*

*Remember, keep your stride short. The bigger your step, the more time it takes to throw.*

**4** As your front foot lands, start bringing your elbow forward quickly. Try to keep the ball close to your head.

**5** Keep your weight going forward as you release the ball. Follow through with your arm across your chest.

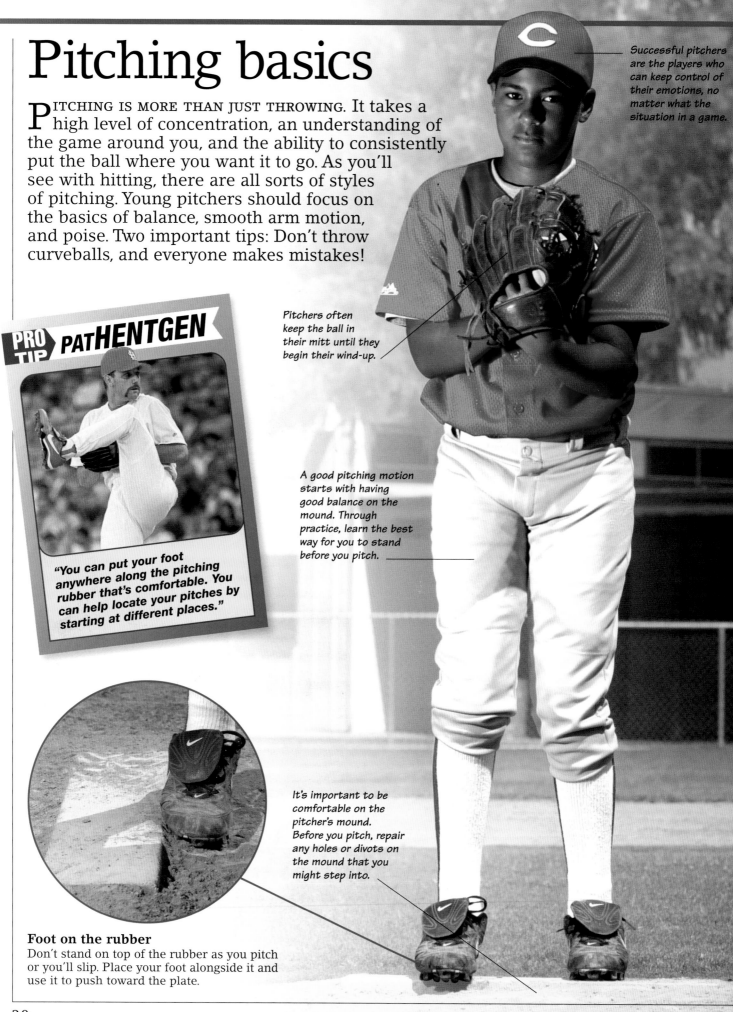

# Pitching basics

PITCHING IS MORE THAN JUST THROWING. It takes a high level of concentration, an understanding of the game around you, and the ability to consistently put the ball where you want it to go. As you'll see with hitting, there are all sorts of styles of pitching. Young pitchers should focus on the basics of balance, smooth arm motion, and poise. Two important tips: Don't throw curveballs, and everyone makes mistakes!

*Successful pitchers are the players who can keep control of their emotions, no matter what the situation in a game.*

*Pitchers often keep the ball in their mitt until they begin their wind-up.*

**PRO TIP** **PATHENTGEN**

*"You can put your foot anywhere along the pitching rubber that's comfortable. You can help locate your pitches by starting at different places."*

*A good pitching motion starts with having good balance on the mound. Through practice, learn the best way for you to stand before you pitch.*

*It's important to be comfortable on the pitcher's mound. Before you pitch, repair any holes or divots on the mound that you might step into.*

## Foot on the rubber
Don't stand on top of the rubber as you pitch or you'll slip. Place your foot alongside it and use it to push toward the plate.

## Path of the pitch
This diagram shows that, if you're pitching from a mound, you're actually throwing "downhill" toward home plate.

## Holding the ball

Pitchers younger than 12 years old should not throw curveballs. Most players' arms are not developed enough to handle the stress on the muscles and joints. There's plenty of time to learn about "breaking pitches" later.

### Fastball
This "four-seam" fastball grip is a good, basic one for young pitchers. This type of fastball rolls out of the hand easily, causing backspin that helps keep the ball straight and low.

### Change-up
Hitters can be fooled by using this pitch, which looks like a fastball, but takes longer to get to the plate. Use this grip and the same arm motion and arm speed as with a fastball.

### Pitcher's glove
As a pitcher, you can use just about any fielder's glove. Many kids play other positions in addition to pitcher, so they use the same glove all the time. Pro pitchers often use a glove like this one. Many pitchers prefer to have their index finger out of the glove as they pitch. It doesn't help their pitching or fielding, they just like it that way.

*Special leather sleeve for pitcher's index finger*

### From pitcher to fielder
As soon as the ball leaves your hand, you go from being pitcher to infielder. You have to be ready for anything: a line drive, a ground ball, a pop-up. Try to finish your delivery with your shoulders square to home plate. That way you can bounce off the mound to make plays like this one.

*Pitching rubber*

*Pitchers use the same technique for catching ground balls as other infielders (see page 16).*

# The delivery

MAJOR LEAGUE PLAYERS MAKE pitching look easy, don't they? They just rear back and fire strike after strike. But they didn't just show up on the mound one day and "throw bee-bees." Over many long practice sessions, they perfected their pitching motion, which many coaches call the "delivery." These pictures show a simple, basic delivery. Work with a coach to develop yours.

**PRO TIP   TROY PERCIVAL**

"You need to learn that you will fail. It's part of the game. Learning that will help you deal with days that don't go right. You have to forget about tough games."

From start to finish, keep your eyes on the target: your catcher's glove.

As your hand comes out of your glove, keep a good, firm grip on the ball. But don't squeeze it like a lemon!

See how his body has pivoted to point his left shoulder at the target?

Reach back with your arm as you pull the ball up.

Try to feel your right foot "dig" into and drive off the rubber.

Help yourself stay balanced by holding your glove hand out.

Your left foot now starts moving forward and your body follows.

**1** The wind-up begins with a small step and the raising of the hands, which are together. Your right foot pivots to the front side of the pitching rubber. (Note: Lefthanders should reverse left-right instructions.) Then pull your left knee up toward your chest.

**2** As your left knee pulls up to your chest, separate your hands at the top of your leg kick. Try to be balanced up-and-down at this point. Then your right hand begins moving backward. As your hand moves back, try to keep your palm down and knuckles up.

**3** Keep bringing your arm back and then up as your body moves forward. Your left foot is important here: Step forward as far as is comfortable. Try to point your toe directly at home plate. Don't step to the right, across your body. Crossing this imaginary center line forces you to throw uncomfortably across your body. Keep your motion going forward at all times.

The circle you've been making with the ball now starts moving toward the plate. Leading with your bent elbow, throw the ball hard toward the target.

After the ball leaves your hand, your palm should be up and your knuckles down.

You should look only at the catcher's mitt, not the batter, as you pitch.

4 As you move toward the target, your pitching hand is above or level with your head and your elbow is bent. Using your shoulder, start pulling your elbow forward quickly. Your forearm, wrist, and hand will follow! As your left foot lands, whip your arm forward. Try to feel your pitches come from your shoulder. Snap your wrist and release the ball from a point slightly in front of you. Finally, listen to your coach about how much to practice. Young arms should be careful not to pitch too much.

Point your chest at the target as you release the ball; try to keep your chest over your front knee.

### What pitcher struck out the most batters?

Nolan Ryan threw his overpowering fastball for four teams during his amazing 27-year career. He struck out 5,714 batters, the most ever. In 1973, he set the modern single-season record when he whiffed 383 hitters.

Push hard off the rubber with your right foot.

Keep your front knee bent for support and to make it easier to move quickly into fielding position.

See how the front foot points the way to the target?

A good way to practice your delivery is to "shadow pitch," or go through your whole delivery without the ball. This helps your body learn the motions, and doesn't overwork your arm.

# More pitching tips

A GOOD PITCHER KNOWS THAT along with his arm, his most important weapon is under his hat. More than any other position, the pitcher needs to use their head. Focus, concentration, and the ability to handle problems are all part of being a successful pitcher.

*In the set position, your shoulders are in line with home plate and second base.*

*Take a glance at the baserunners, then look in for your target.*

*Start with your hands about chest high, then drop them down as you pick up your left knee to begin the delivery.*

*Stay balanced, with more of your weight on your back leg as you set up.*

## Listen up

During a game, your coach might visit you on the mound to give you advice or talk about the hitter. These breaks in the action are a good time to take a deep breath and focus your mind.

### Who gave up the most home runs?

Don't worry about giving up hits and home runs. Phillies pitcher Robin Roberts gave up an all-time record 505 round-trippers in his career, but he still wound up with 286 career wins and a spot in the Hall of Fame. Good pitchers know that conquering their fears and worries makes them stronger on the mound.

## The set position

Pro pitchers use this delivery instead of a wind-up whenever there are men on base. The set position delivers the ball to the plate more quickly, giving baserunners less of a jump. Instead of rocking back before stepping toward home, begin with your foot right next to the rubber, go directly into your leg kick, and drive toward home.

*From the set position you still push off the rubber as you pitch.*

# COVERING FIRST BASE

Along with fielding grounders and backing up bases on throws from the outfield, the pitcher's most important defensive job is covering first base when the ball is hit to the first baseman. Pitchers need to instantly break for first whenever the ball is hit in that direction.

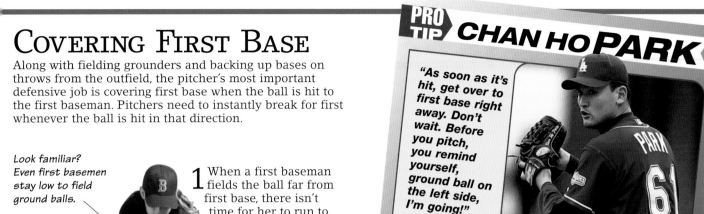

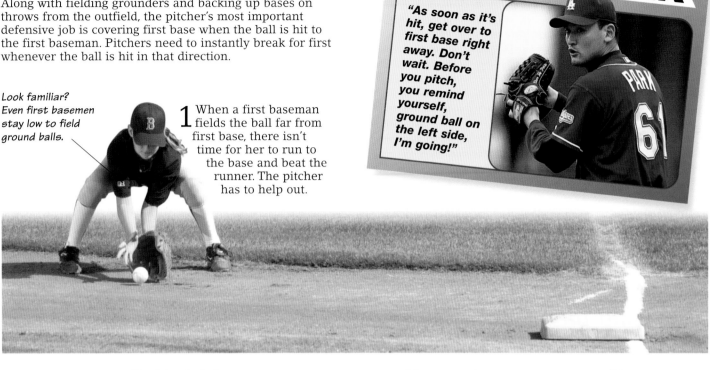

*Look familiar? Even first basemen stay low to field ground balls.*

**1** When a first baseman fields the ball far from first base, there isn't time for her to run to the base and beat the runner. The pitcher has to help out.

*Watch for the ball first, then look for the base.*

*Run toward the inside part of the first base bag.*

*After you catch it, keep running, tag the base, and get out of the way!*

*Use the base to push off toward the field and away from the baseline.*

**2** The pitcher breaks toward the base and gives the first baseman a target. The first baseman should aim for a spot between the pitcher and the base. As the pitcher heads toward the bag, he should run parallel to the baseline.

**3** Be sure to make the catch first; that's the most important thing. Then touch the inside part of the base and push off toward the field. Don't run across the bag or you might have a collision with the baserunner.

# Batting basics

MARK MCGWIRE CALLS BATTING "the hardest thing to do in sports." If you've ever tried to hit a fast-moving round ball with a round bat, then you know what he's talking about. But batting is like any skill; with knowledge of the basics and practice, you can steadily improve and become a good hitter. There are just as many theories about hitting as there are players. On these pages, you'll read the basics. The rest is up to you; the only real way to become a better hitter is to do what the pros do: practice, practice, practice.

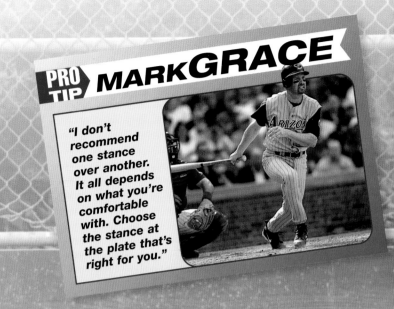

PRO TIP **MARKGRACE**

"I don't recommend one stance over another. It all depends on what you're comfortable with. Choose the stance at the plate that's right for you."

*Don't forget to always wear your batting helmet with double ear flaps.*

## Lefties and righties

Players bat from one side of home plate or the other. If your left foot is closest to the pitcher when you're in your stance, you are a righthanded batter. If your right foot is closest, you're batting lefthanded. Though switch hitting (batting from either side) is fun to try, concentrate on your strongest side first.

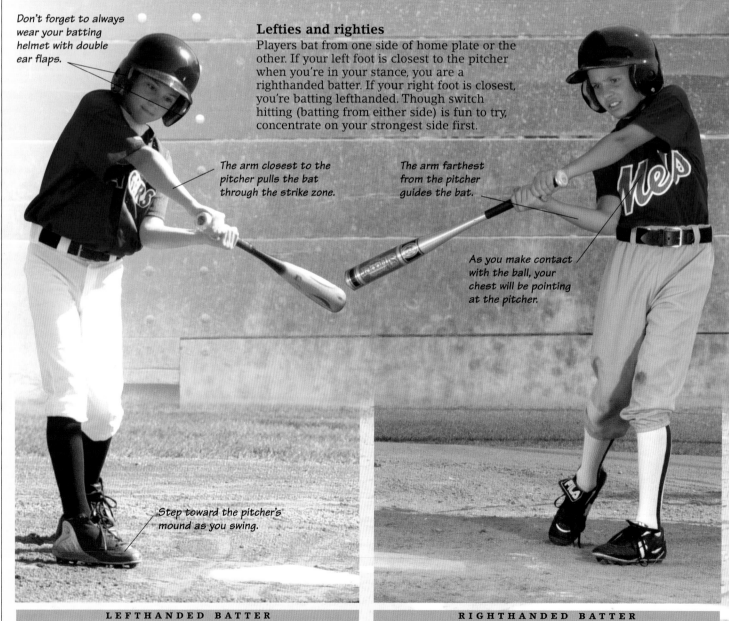

*The arm closest to the pitcher pulls the bat through the strike zone.*

*The arm farthest from the pitcher guides the bat.*

*As you make contact with the ball, your chest will be pointing at the pitcher.*

*Step toward the pitcher's mound as you swing.*

LEFTHANDED BATTER

RIGHTHANDED BATTER

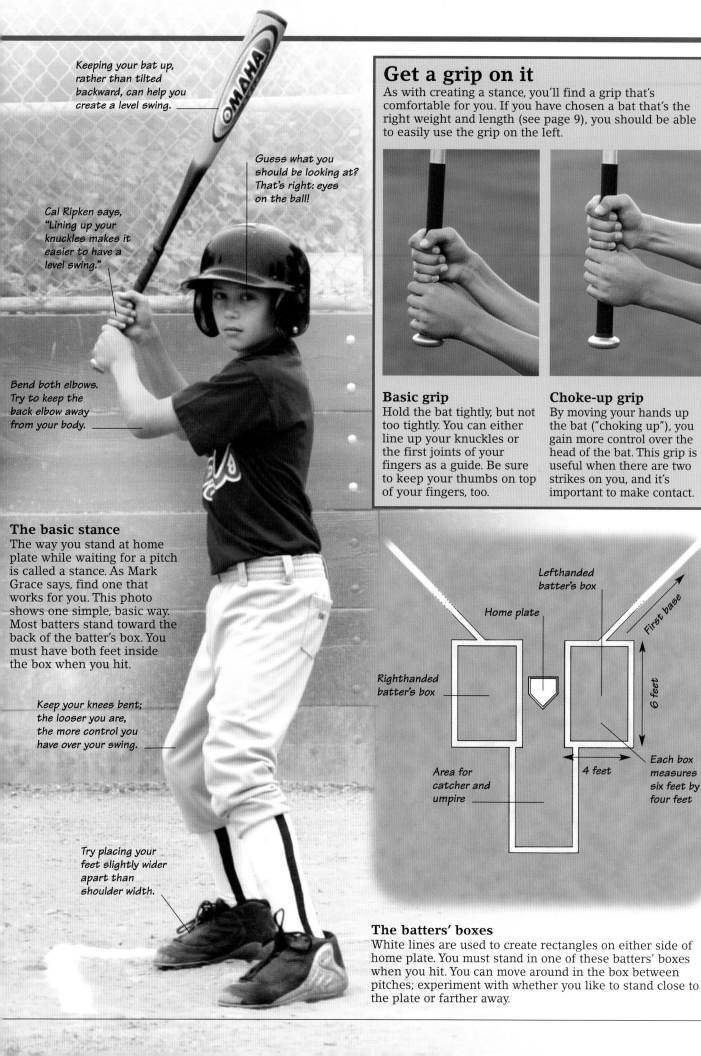

Keeping your bat up, rather than tilted backward, can help you create a level swing.

Cal Ripken says, "Lining up your knuckles makes it easier to have a level swing."

Guess what you should be looking at? That's right: eyes on the ball!

Bend both elbows. Try to keep the back elbow away from your body.

## Get a grip on it

As with creating a stance, you'll find a grip that's comfortable for you. If you have chosen a bat that's the right weight and length (see page 9), you should be able to easily use the grip on the left.

### Basic grip

Hold the bat tightly, but not too tightly. You can either line up your knuckles or the first joints of your fingers as a guide. Be sure to keep your thumbs on top of your fingers, too.

### Choke-up grip

By moving your hands up the bat ("choking up"), you gain more control over the head of the bat. This grip is useful when there are two strikes on you, and it's important to make contact.

## The basic stance

The way you stand at home plate while waiting for a pitch is called a stance. As Mark Grace says, find one that works for you. This photo shows one simple, basic way. Most batters stand toward the back of the batter's box. You must have both feet inside the box when you hit.

Keep your knees bent; the looser you are, the more control you have over your swing.

Try placing your feet slightly wider apart than shoulder width.

Lefthanded batter's box

Home plate

First base

Righthanded batter's box

6 feet

Each box measures six feet by four feet

Area for catcher and umpire

4 feet

## The batters' boxes

White lines are used to create rectangles on either side of home plate. You must stand in one of these batters' boxes when you hit. You can move around in the box between pitches; experiment with whether you like to stand close to the plate or farther away.

# The swing

Y OU'VE GOT YOUR BAT. You've got your grip and your stance. Now comes the tricky part. A basic baseball swing has several parts, any one of which can go wrong at any time. The key is to create a smooth motion from your first step toward the pitcher all the way to your follow-through. This page shows a simple, basic swing. Yours might look different; as players will tell you, it's the results that count.

## Common mistakes
Many young players make similar mistakes at the plate. Here are two of the hitting problems that youth coaches see most often.

Home plate

**Stepping "in the bucket"**
If you step away from home plate instead of toward the pitcher, you fall away from the ball, lose power, and have little chance of getting a hit. Focus on moving your foot and body toward the pitcher.

**Pulling your head out**
You can't hit what you can't see. If you are looking away from the ball and the plate, as this player shows, you are giving the pitcher a huge edge. We can't say it enough: Keep your eyes on the ball.

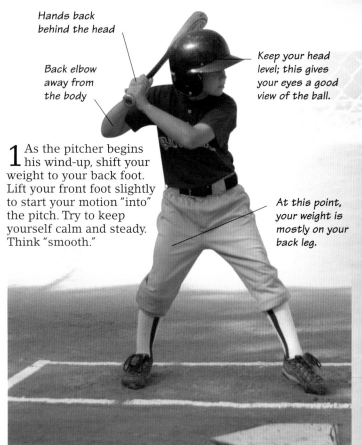

Hands back behind the head

Back elbow away from the body

Keep your head level; this gives your eyes a good view of the ball.

**1** As the pitcher begins his wind-up, shift your weight to your back foot. Lift your front foot slightly to start your motion "into" the pitch. Try to keep yourself calm and steady. Think "smooth."

At this point, your weight is mostly on your back leg.

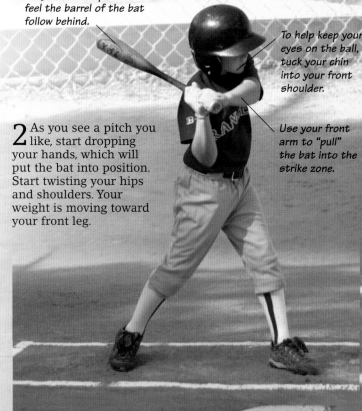

As your hands pull forward, feel the barrel of the bat follow behind.

To help keep your eyes on the ball, tuck your chin into your front shoulder.

**2** As you see a pitch you like, start dropping your hands, which will put the bat into position. Start twisting your hips and shoulders. Your weight is moving toward your front leg.

Use your front arm to "pull" the bat into the strike zone.

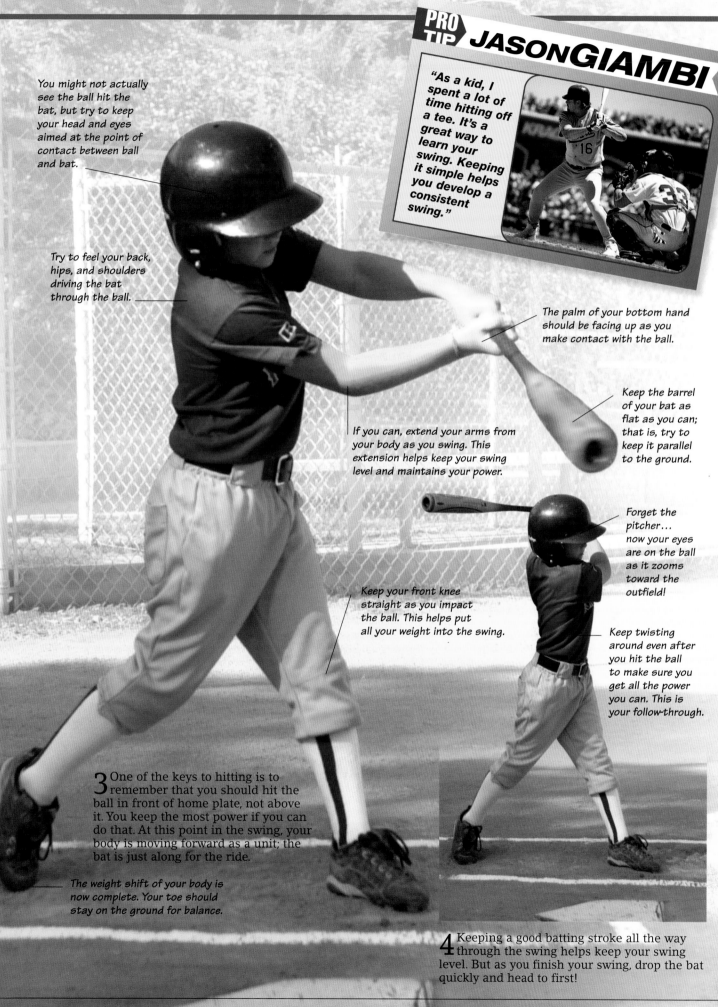

You might not actually see the ball hit the bat, but try to keep your head and eyes aimed at the point of contact between ball and bat.

Try to feel your back, hips, and shoulders driving the bat through the ball.

## JASONGIAMBI

"As a kid, I spent a lot of time hitting off a tee. It's a great way to learn your swing. Keeping it simple helps you develop a consistent swing."

The palm of your bottom hand should be facing up as you make contact with the ball.

If you can, extend your arms from your body as you swing. This extension helps keep your swing level and maintains your power.

Keep the barrel of your bat as flat as you can; that is, try to keep it parallel to the ground.

Forget the pitcher... now your eyes are on the ball as it zooms toward the outfield!

Keep your front knee straight as you impact the ball. This helps put all your weight into the swing.

Keep twisting around even after you hit the ball to make sure you get all the power you can. This is your follow-through.

3 One of the keys to hitting is to remember that you should hit the ball in front of home plate, not above it. You keep the most power if you can do that. At this point in the swing, your body is moving forward as a unit; the bat is just along for the ride.

The weight shift of your body is now complete. Your toe should stay on the ground for balance.

4 Keeping a good batting stroke all the way through the swing helps keep your swing level. But as you finish your swing, drop the bat quickly and head to first!

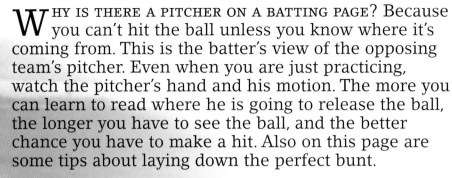

# More batting tips

*The pitcher's hand is moving toward the release point.*

WHY IS THERE A PITCHER ON A BATTING PAGE? Because you can't hit the ball unless you know where it's coming from. This is the batter's view of the opposing team's pitcher. Even when you are just practicing, watch the pitcher's hand and his motion. The more you can learn to read where he is going to release the ball, the longer you have to see the ball, and the better chance you have to make a hit. Also on this page are some tips about laying down the perfect bunt.

## BUNTING

Bunting is an important skill that not enough players practice. A good bunt can kick-start a team's offense.

*At the start of your at-bat, hold your bat as if you're up there to make a full swing.*

### Follow the ball
Every pitcher you face will have a slightly different wind-up and delivery. But they will all have a "release point." This is the place in space in which the ball leaves the pitching hand. Focus on that spot more than on the pitcher's body, and you'll increase your chances for batting success.

*Stay loose and on your toes with your knees bent. You'll need to be ready to move your feet quickly into position.*

1 After you've gotten the bunt signal from your coach, think about what you're going to do as the pitcher begins his wind-up.

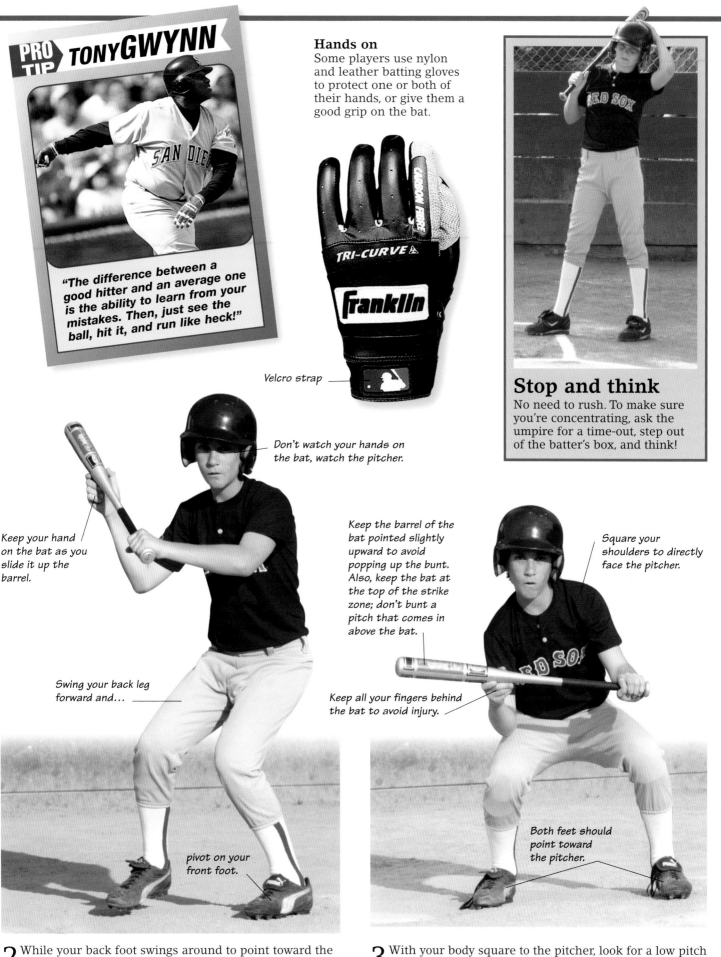

## Hands on
Some players use nylon and leather batting gloves to protect one or both of their hands, or give them a good grip on the bat.

TRI-CURVE

CARBON FIBRE

Franklin

Velcro strap

## Stop and think
No need to rush. To make sure you're concentrating, ask the umpire for a time-out, step out of the batter's box, and think!

Don't watch your hands on the bat, watch the pitcher.

Keep your hand on the bat as you slide it up the barrel.

Swing your back leg forward and...

pivot on your front foot.

Keep the barrel of the bat pointed slightly upward to avoid popping up the bunt. Also, keep the bat at the top of the strike zone; don't bunt a pitch that comes in above the bat.

Keep all your fingers behind the bat to avoid injury.

Square your shoulders to directly face the pitcher.

Both feet should point toward the pitcher.

2 While your back foot swings around to point toward the pitcher, move your top hand up the barrel of the bat. Start pivoting your body to face the pitcher.

3 With your body square to the pitcher, look for a low pitch and try to "catch" the ball with the bat. Don't poke or swing. The aim is to make the ball drop just a few feet away.

# Baserunning basics

A PLAYER'S JOB ISN'T OVER once he reaches base. It's actually beginning again, as he turns from batter to baserunner. The key to baserunning, as Darin Erstad says, is "run hard." You should also always know how many outs there are and what the count is. For instance, with two outs, run hard on any hit. Try to be aware of what you should do as a baserunner no matter where the ball is hit.

## LEADING OFF

If your league allows you to lead off bases, practice getting a safe lead and a good "jump" when the ball is hit.

"Run hard. One thing you can always control and that's hustle. It doesn't take much effort to run hard. The base isn't that far away."

Stay on your toes and be ready to run at all times.

**1** Take two or three steps from the base, and face home plate, but keep your eyes on the pitcher. As soon as he throws home, look at the batter.

Use your arms to help you get started.

Make your first, or "crossover", step using the leg closest to first base.

**2** As the ball is hit, start running hard toward second. If it's a ground ball, go hard into the base. If it's a fly ball, wait and see where it's hit.

## Another way to go

Some leagues don't allow leading off. In that case, plant your foot on the base and face second base. That way, you're ready to run at the crack of the bat.

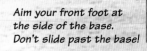

Aim your front foot at the side of the base. Don't slide past the base!

# Coaches' signals

Whether it's your coach or your teammate in the third-base coaches' box, it's important for you as a baserunner to do what they signal. Baserunners should concentrate on running hard and looking ahead. Coaches can see the whole field; they'll tell you what to do.

Keep your arms and hands in the air to avoid jamming them into the ground.

### Stop!
Don't go farther than the base you're on or the base you're heading to. You don't have to slide.

### Slide!
Get ready to slide as you reach the base. The coach can see a throw coming in behind you.

### Keep going!
This is the best signal to see. Touch the base and keep running. If you're heading home, look ahead for a teammate for more help.

### Slide, kid, slide!
As you approach the base, tuck one leg underneath your butt and point the other toward the base. Slide on your calf and outer thigh. Sliding can be hard to master. Try practicing on grass first; you can even use a slip-and-slide to practice on.

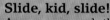

Keep your front leg slightly bent to absorb impact.

### Rounding the base
Don't step on the middle of the bag. Step on the corner pointing to the pitcher's mound as you move past the base.

Tuck your foot under you. This helps cushion the impact of landing on dirt.

You can slide with either foot forward. Practice with both feet to find which is more comfortable for you. Most players put their right foot forward, but the left works just fine, too.

Some players wear special baseball sliding shorts under their uniform pants. These stretch-fit shorts have thin pads that help cushion the impact of sliding.

# Have fun!

WE HOPE YOU HAVE ENJOYED reading about how to be a better baseball player. As the Major League players all said, the key to success is practice and hard work. Having a good attitude is important, too. Winning is great, but trying hard, working on your skills, and helping your team are even more important. Now go out there and have fun!

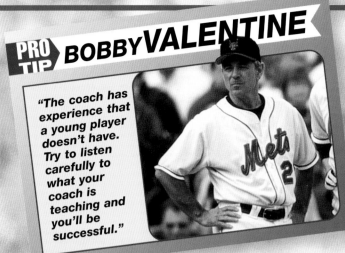
**How can you join a team?**
Ask your parents to look in your local phone book for a youth baseball organization near you. Most leagues play in the spring and offer teams for players of all ages and abilities. Your parents will sign you up, and you'll be assigned to a team.

## The joy of victory

The players celebrating here have just won the Little League World Series, held each August since 1947 in Williamsport, Pennsylvania. Little League is the largest youth baseball organization in the world, with more than 3 million boys and girls playing in more than 100 countries. To reach the World Series, all-star teams of 11–12-year-olds are chosen from local leagues. They then compete in local and regional tournaments. Eight winners from the U.S. and eight international winners advance to Williamsport for the Series. The final is televised nationwide, creating memories that will last a lifetime.

## Listen up

Your team will have coaches whose job is to help you have fun, be safe, and play better. Listen carefully to what they say; they're on your side.

## Sportsmanship rules

Even after a hard-fought game, make sure to shake your opponents' hands. Demonstrate sportsmanship, just like these Little League World Series participants.

# Thanks, guys!

On these pages, read more about the Major League players who passed along some "tips from the pros" in this book. They're pro players today, but, remember, they were young players once, too, just like you. Work hard and you never know…

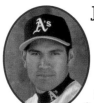

### Johnny Damon
**OUTFIELD, OAKLAND ATHLETICS**
A top leadoff hitter must combine speed with batting skill—Johnny has both. In six seasons with the Kansas City Royals, he stole 25 or more bases four times, including a league-leading 46 in 2000.
*See page 18.*

### Darin Erstad
**OUTFIELD, ANAHEIM ANGELS**
Darin brings all-around athletic skill to the diamond. In college, he was the punter on Nebraska's national champion football team. In 2000, he had an awesome season, batting .355 with a league-leading 240 hits.
*See pages 25, 42.*

### Nomar Garciaparra
**SHORTSTOP, BOSTON RED SOX**
This two-time A.L. batting champ is one of baseball's best players. A three-time All-Star, he helped Boston reach the playoffs twice. (To invent "Nomar," father Ramon spelled his own name backward!)
*See page 20.*

### Jason Giambi
**FIRST BASE/DH, OAKLAND ATHLETICS**
Talk about steady improvement: Jason increased his batting average in each of his first six pro seasons. In 2000, he was named the A.L. MV. He also has helped Oakland make the playoffs twice.
*See page 39.*

### Mark Grace
**FIRST BASE, ARIZONA DIAMONDBACKS**
No Major League player had more hits or doubles in the 1990s than Mark Grace. With the Cubs, he had nine seasons above .300 and won three Gold Gloves. He helped Arizona win the 2001 World Series.
*See page 36.*

### Rusty Greer
**OUTFIELD, TEXAS RANGERS**
Many scouts thought Rusty wouldn't make it in the big leagues, but he proved them wrong. He has batted .300 or better five times and has three seasons of 100-plus RBI. (His real name? Thurman Clyde!)
*See page 24.*

### Tony Gwynn
**OUTFIELD, SAN DIEGO PADRES**
Tony is simply one of the finest hitters in baseball history. In his 23-year career with the Padres, he won eight N.L. batting titles, tying for the most ever. A 16-time All-Star, he hit .300 or better in 18 seasons.
*See page 41.*

### Pat Hentgen
**PITCHER, ST. LOUIS CARDINALS**
Pat was a consistent, durable starter for the Toronto Blue Jays from 1991–99. His best season was 1996, when he won 20 games and the Cy Young Award. He joined the Cardinals in 2000, winning 15 games.
*See page 30.*

### Derek Jeter
**SHORTSTOP, NEW YORK YANKEES**
Though he's only 26 years old, Derek already boasts four World Series rings and a position as the Yankees' team leader. Derek was the MVP of the All-Star Game and the World Series in 2000.
*See page 16.*

### Rey Ordoñez
**SHORTSTOP, NEW YORK METS**
Rey is a native of Cuba and is also one of the most exciting fielders in baseball. His diving catches, leaping grabs, and amazing glovework routinely make the highlight shows, helping him win three Gold Gloves.
*See page 14.*

### Chan Ho Park
**PITCHER, LOS ANGELES DODGERS**
Chan Ho is the first native of Korea to succeed in the Major Leagues. He joined the Dodgers' starting rotation in 1996. His great fastball has helped him post five straight winning seasons.
*See page 35.*

### Troy Percival
**PITCHER, ANAHEIM ANGELS**
As the Angels' closer, Troy has become one of baseball's most feared pitchers. His overpowering fastball and nasty curveball have helped him save at least 30 games in five different seasons.
*See page 32.*

## Mike Piazza
**CATCHER, NEW YORK METS**
Mike is the best-hitting catcher in Major
League history, with a .325 career average.
He helped the Mets reach the 2000 World
Series. Mike starred on the Los Angeles
Dodgers from 1992–98.
*See pages 6, 26.*

## Cal Ripken, Jr.
**THIRD BASE, BALTIMORE ORIOLES**
A record streak of 2,632 consecutive
games played is just one of dozens of
highlights for this two-time MVP and
19-time All-Star. Cal, who helped the O's
win the 1983 World Series, retired in 2001.
*See page 8.*

## Tim Salmon
**OUTFIELD, ANAHEIM ANGELS**
Tim not only has one of the most
powerful outfield arms in baseball,
he's also a top slugger. He was the
1993 Rookie of the Year, and he has 5
seasons of 30-plus home runs.
*See pages 10, 22.*

## Bobby Valentine
**MANAGER, NEW YORK METS**
A former outfielder with four teams,
Bobby managed the Texas Rangers from
1985–92. He took over the Mets in 1996
and has led them to the playoffs twice,
including a spot in the 2000 World Series.
*See page 44.*

## Robin Ventura
**THIRD BASE, NEW YORK METS**
One of the greatest college players in
history, Robin had a 58-game hitting
streak at Oklahoma State. His 12-year
Major League career, with the White Sox
and Mets, has included six Gold Gloves.
*See page 12.*

## Rick Wilkins
**CATCHER, SAN DIEGO PADRES**
A solid defensive catcher with a
dependable lefthanded bat, Rick has
played for eight teams in his 11-year
career which began with the Cubs in 1991.
He has played in the A.L. and N.L. playoffs.
*See page 28.*

# MORE WAYS TO "PLAY BALL!"

We hope this book has given you a good introduction to
basic baseball skills and inspired you to enjoy playing
the game. But there's a lot more to enjoy about baseball,
both on the field and off. Here are some books and Web
sites you can check out to learn more about the game
and to take the next steps in your baseball development.
Look at your local bookstore or library for these and
other baseball books. And ask your parents for help (if
you need it!) browsing baseball Web sites.

## BOOKS
***Baseball Top 10*** (DK Publishing, 2002)
This book of "Top 10" lists is filled with more stats than
you can shake a bat at, from the greatest players and
teams of yesterday to today's top stars.

***Visual Dictionary of Baseball*** (DK Publishing, 2001)
Talk the talk with this picture-filled dictionary about
every aspect of baseball, including details on
equipment, history, stats, cards, and more.

***Eyewitness Baseball*** (DK Publishing, 1999)
Want to see up-close pictures of real Major League
gear? Learn about baseball's early days? Find out more
about baseball in other countries? You can do all that
and more in this 64-page book, full of great color
pictures and diagrams.

***DK/MLB Readers*** (DK Publishing, 1999)
Young baseball fans can learn about Major League
stars past and present while practicing their reading
skills with these four great baseball readers: *Roberto
Clemente*, *Home Run Heroes*, *Super Shortstops*, and
*Strikeout Kings*.

## WEB SITES
***www.mlb.com*** *(below)*
The official Web site of Major League Baseball is packed
with great information on all your favorite Major League
players. You can also read the official rules of the game,
check out stats and stories from baseball's past, and
create a personalized video highlight package of your
favorite players.

***www.littleleague.org/kids***
This part of the official Little League Baseball site has
online baseball games, plus links to other Little League
sites that tell about the Little League World Series,
official rules, and information about equipment.

*Note: Players are listed with their 2001 teams.*

# Index

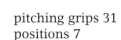

# Acknowledgments

Thanks first of all to our excellent baseball models (and their very patient parents!) from Santa Barbara, California: Gray Clevenger, Kristen Dealy, Timothy Egan, Sean Heiduk, Daniel Motyer, Britney Pintard, Cameron Reid, Daniel Richardson, and Selwyn Young. (Bonus thanks to Denise Heiduk and Dave Pintard for helping us with field and equipment access.)

Thanks to all the Major League Baseball players who contributed their words of wisdom and expertise to help young ballplayers develop and improve. Thanks to Rich Pilling and Paul Cunningham of Major League Baseball Photos.

Special thanks to David Jones of Russell Corporation for graciously donating all of the official Major League Baseball licensed gear worn by the models. Caps were provided by the New Era Cap Co. Thanks to Wilson Sporting Goods and Franklin Sporting Goods for photographs of their gear.

Thanks to Bill Pintard of the Anaheim Angels and Santa Barbara Foresters for his expert advice on pitching; to Beth Sutinis and Michelle Baxter at DK for shepherding this process. Special thanks to designer Tom Carling for perservering through events in New York to finish on time.

Finally, thanks to Conor Buckley, future Red Sox star and my personal assistant at all of our photo shoots.

# Photo Credits

All instructional photography copyright © 2001 by Mike Eliason. Illustrations by George Cheney.

Player photographs copyright © 2001 as listed below.

6  Mike Piazza by Rich Pilling/MLB Photos
8  Cal Ripken by Rich Pilling/MLB Photos
11  Tim Salmon by AP/Wide World
12  Robin Ventura by Allen Kee/MLB Photos
14  Rey Ordoñez by Jeff Carlick/ MLB Photos
16  Derek Jeter by Rich Pilling/ MLB Photos
18  Johnny Damon by Michael Zagaris/MLB Photos
20  Nomar Garciaparra by Allen Kee/MLB Photos
22  Tim Salmon by AP/Wide World
24  Rusty Greer by Michael Zagaris/MLB Photos
26  Mike Piazza by Rich Pilling/MLB Photos
28  Rick Wilkins by AP/Wide World
30  Pat Hentgen by AP/Wide World
32  Troy Percival by Michael Zagaris/MLB Photos
35  Chan Ho Park by Don Smith/MLB Photos
36  Mark Grace by Ron Vesely/MLB Photos
39  Jason Giambi by Brad Mangin/MLB Photos
41  Tony Gwynn by Don Smith/MLB Photos
42  Darin Erstad by David Durochick/MLB Photos
44  Bobby Valentine by Rich Pilling/MLB Photos
44  Little League World Series (2) by AP/Wide World

All player photos on pages 46–47 courtesy MLB Photos.